12174

Crazy – but True

D0809789

This Armada book belongs to:

_____

_____

_____

CRAZY

Jonathan Clements

BUT TRUE!

with drawings by Roger Smith

ARMADA

An Armada Original

Crazy – but True! was first published in 1974
by Wm Collins Sons & Co Ltd,
14 St James's Place, London, SW1

© Jonathan Clements 1974

Printed in Great Britain by
William Collins Sons & Co Ltd, Glasgow

CONDITIONS OF SALE
This book is sold subject to the condition
that it shall not, by way of trade or otherwise,
be lent, re-sold, hired out or otherwise circulated
without the publisher's prior consent in any form of
binding or cover other than that in which it is
published and without a similar condition
including this condition being imposed
on the subsequent purchaser.

Contents

How to be Best at Everything Without Doing Anything

To be extremely popular (and maybe even regarded as a budding genius) is dead easy. All you really have to do is talk to people. But a great deal depends on what you actually *say*. This is where the art of telling freakish facts comes in – curious items of information that can make folk stare boggle-eyed with wonder at you.

And that's where this valuable little book can help you, with its fund of weird and wonderful revelations. Be sure to choose just *what* you say to *whom* very carefully, though. It's no good telling your natural science teacher that snakes hear through their jaws. He won't be impressed –

he'll already know. So here's a few suggestions as to whom you should inform about what:

To a Parent: 'Guess what, Dad – elephants have hardly any memory at all!'

To a History Teacher: 'The musical key of the siren on the liner *Queen Elizabeth* is lower bass A, sir!'

To your Uncle: 'Ladybirds aren't birds. They're beetles!'

To your Auntie: 'The smallest state in the world is Vatican City (180 acres), an enclave within the city of Rome, Italy!'

To a Friend: 'Ice-cream was invented in 1620!'

To an Enemy: 'An insect whose head has been cut off may live as long as a year. So watch it!'

Elsewhere in this book, by the way, you'll find a whole chapter devoted to the many and varied uses of these and other startling facts. All the items of information given are completely true, including the ones above. In this first chapter you'll find a sampling of the treats in store. For example, did you know that . . .

Sealing wax contains no wax. It is made of shellac, turpentine, and cinnabar.

Snakes hear through their jaws.

The motto of the peace-loving Salvation Army is 'Blood and Fire!'

In 1931, the official documents of the Italian Government were printed on glossy paper – the glazing was made of Cornish china clay. When war broke out in 1939, the documents were stored in a damp cellar in Rome. After the war, when the documents were retrieved, the dampness had turned over a million pages of governmental records to solid blocks of Cornish china clay.

Cat gut has nothing to do with cats at all. It comes from sheep.

Up till 1900, café-owners near Stonehenge hired tourists hammers and chisels so they could chip off a piece of the famous monument as a souvenir.

There is no lead in a lead pencil. The material used is either plumbago or graphite, a form of carbon.

Giraffes have no voices.

A ton of coal is needed to produce a ton of paper.

The Church clock at Wootton Rivers, in Wiltshire, is made of old bedsteads, bicycles and pram frames. It is in working order, and keeps perfect time.

Tantalum, a metallic chemical element, is the hardest of all the stones – even harder than the diamond.

An electric fan doesn't cool the air of the room in which it is operating. A thermometer held in the current of air caused by the fan will not register a lower temperature. The fan cools the skin by increasing evaporation of perspiration, thereby producing a feeling of comfort.

Chinese proverb: Wash face in the morning and neck at night.

Peter Labellière expressed his criticism of the world by leaving in his will the direction to bury him head downwards. This, he explained, 'is because the world is topsy-turvy, and it is fit that I be so buried that I might be right at last.' Labellière's instructions were carried out. He died in June, 1800, and was buried at Box Hill in Surrey, where his small gravestone can still be seen.

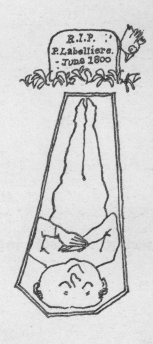

George Washington's great-great-grandfather was a student of Brasenose College, Oxford. When he left Oxford, he owed a food bill of eight shillings. The three-hundred year old debt was finally paid by American soldiers stationed at Oxford during World War I.

Researchers in Denmark found that beer tastes best when drunk to the accompaniment of a certain musical tone. The sound range is different for each beer. The correct harmonious tone for lager, for example, is 540–520 cycles per second.

Elephants, despite their reputation for never forgetting anything, have hardly any memory at all.

Flying fish don't fly at all. Their long pectoral fins, when distended at high speed, merely give that illusion.

In Japan, Santa Claus isn't a jolly old man – he's a jolly old woman.

Ice-cream was invented in 1620 by a French chef named Gerald Tissain; he was granted a life pension of £20 a year by King Charles I for his noble deed. But when Charles lost his head to the executioner's axe, Tissain also lost his pension.

A raisin, dropped into a glass of champagne, will rise and fall *forever* in the glass.

The scientist Hegel published his proof that there could be no more than seven planets just a week before the discovery of the eighth.

Cocoa grows on cacao trees, not on cocoa trees.

Black isn't the universal colour for mourning the dead. South Sea Islanders wear red; Ethiopians wear brown; Egyptians wear yellow; and the people of Turkey wear violet.

The three body segments of an insect do not depend on one another for survival. Thus an insect whose head has been cut off may live as long as a year in this condition.

The word FACETIOUSLY contains all the vowels arranged in their correct alphabetical order.

Indian ink doesn't come from India, but from China. It is made from lamp-black and gum.

The expression 'It's all Greek to me!' was originated by William Shakespeare in his play *Julius Caesar* (Act 1 Scene 2, line 289).

There is no kid in kid gloves. They are made of lambskin or sheepskin.

Alan Lerner took two weeks to write the last line of the song 'Wouldn't It Be Loverly?' for the show *My Fair Lady*. The words of the last line are: 'Loverly, loverly, loverly, loverly.'

The twentieth century began on January 1st, 1901 (not on January 1st 1900).

The ladybird isn't a bird. It's a beetle.

The musical key of the siren on the liner *Queen Elizabeth* is lower bass A.

The average man spends 3,500 hours of his life on shaving. In this time, he removes about 30 ft of whiskers off his face.

The reason sardines are crammed so tightly into their tins is that the oil used to pack them is more expensive by volume than the fish themselves. Thus, the more sardines the manufacturer can squeeze into a tin, the greater his profit.

In 1897, while serving a sentence in the Ohio State Penitentiary, a prisoner named Charles Justice helped design, build and install its first electric chair. Years later, he returned to the prison after being convicted of murder. In 1911, Charles Justice was executed in the same electric chair.

How to Escape from Extremely Perilous Situations

Say you're trapped under a steam-roller that's just about to start moving. (Go on, say it! it doesn't hurt.) Well, what do you do? The most normal reaction would be to faint with fear. But undoubtedly the best way out of this predicament is to shout something strange and compelling, such as: 'An ostrich egg takes forty minutes to boil!' This will stop everybody in their tracks, and you'll be saved from the fate of being rolled out flat and fantastically thin. Which proves the value of curious information – if you can come up with something really incredible-sounding (such as: 'Deer have no gall bladders!'), then people will stop and listen.

This technique can also be used if you're in the clutches of desperate enemies. When in their fiendish power, just act cool and hiss through your gag: 'Set me free and I'll tell you how many times a fly's wings vibrate every second . . .' Who could possibly go through life ignorant of such a fascinating fact? (You'll find the answer in this very chapter.) Also included in this chapter are priceless lumps of information which will help you climb down chimneys, scale mountains, fight bare-fisted with man-eating tigers, escape from sinking ships and navigate a course through alligator-infested jungles. We won't spoil your fun by telling you which is which – you work it out.

An ostrich egg takes approximately forty minutes to soft-boil. And an hour and a half to hard-boil.

Jumping beans have real live fleas inside them.

A salmon's age can only be determined by the number of lines on its jawbone.

The longest word in the English language is not, as most people seem to think:
'ANTIDISESTABLISHMENTARIANISM'
This is just a junior at 28 letters long. The record is in fact a word that's 45 letters long, describing a lung disease, namely:
'PNEUMONOULTRAMISCROSCOPICICSILICO-VOLCANOCONIOSIS'

Mozart wrote the music of 'Twinkle, Twinkle Little Star' at the age of five.

There is a small village in France named 'Y'.

There is no word in English that rhymes with 'orange'.

In April, 1906, a head-on collision occurred in Redruth, Cornwall. So what? The accident was between the only two cars existing in the town at the time.

It takes 1,204 Italian centessimi to equal one English penny.

It was extremely expensive to send a letter or a parcel in the old days. For instance, in America in 1880, the Pony Express rates worked out at roughly £3·50 an ounce.

The very first set of false teeth were made of wood (elm) and were worn by George Washington.

It is against the law to ride on a bus in Indiana, U.S.A., within four hours of eating garlic.

Deer have no gall bladders.

The famous London market Petticoat Lane is not held in Petticoat Lane, but in Middlesex Street. The market's nickname comes from the 18th century, when mostly ladies clothing was sold there.

Seven and a half million tons of water evaporate from the Dead Sea every day.

Bulls are colour-blind.

Upon being crowned Queen of England, Victoria's very first royal proclamation was a command that all her dogs be given a hot bath. Queen Victoria owned up to eighty dogs at a time, and knew them all by name.

Greenland, with a population of 35,000, has no telephones.

A fly's wings vibrate 340 times a second.

Over half the contents of a grebe's stomach consists of feathers.

Alfred Nobel, who initiated and sponsored the famous Nobel Peace Prize, invented dynamite.

The bicycle was invented in 1840 by a certain Fitzpatrick Macmillan. Some months before this, Macmillan had been fined fifteen shillings for recklessly driving his horse and carriage.

King Louis XIV of France originated and was the first to wear high-heeled shoes.

The expression 'mind your P's and Q's' derives, not from 'please and thank you', but from 'Pints and Quarts', an expression used by suspicious brewers in the nineteenth century.

There are only twelve letters in the Hawaiian alphabet: A—E—H—I—K—L—M—N—O—P—U—W.

Pineapples aren't apples or pines. They're large berries.

It is impossible to sneeze
with your eyes open.

The famous Elizabethan poet Ben Jonson is buried in a
sitting position in Poet's Corner at Westminster Abbey, for
the plot provided for him wasn't large enough for the
corpse to be placed horizontally.

Spaghetti, contrary to popular belief, did not originate in
Italy, but in China. It was first discovered on one of Marco
Polo's voyages.

Benjamin Franklin invented the rocking chair.

A thousand years from now the population of the world
is expected to equal the number of pounds of earth that
exist.

Brazil used to print a bank note worth one cruzeiro. It was discontinued in 1960, when it was accidentally discovered that it cost one and a half cruzeiros to print.

Ju-jitsu, literally translated into English, means 'The gentle art'.

There is no cork in the artificial leg known as a cork leg. The name comes from Dr Cork, who invented them.

George IV of England's cause of death was officially recorded as: rupture of the stomach blood vessels; alcoholic cirrhosis; gout; nephritis, and dropsy.

The Great Dane breed of dog doesn't come from Denmark, but from Germany, where it is known as a German Boarhound.

Despite the expression 'crocodile tears', crocodiles never cry or shed tears.

The first ever 'Wish-you-were here' holiday greetings card to be sent was posted in 1866 by the infamous Wild West sharpshooter, Annie Oakley.

The 'X' in 'Xmas', the abbreviated expression for Christmas, represents the first letter of Christ's name in Greek. The term originated in the Middle Ages.

Author Robert Louis Stevenson wrote his classic *Travels On a Donkey* whilst on his honeymoon.

A Short but Exciting History of Black Treacle

f you look closely at the label on a tin of black treacle, ou'll see that it's called *green* treacle. And if you open the in and scoop out some with a spoon, you'll find that the reacle is actually *brown* in colour. (If you do all this you'll robably get covered in treacle as well, but never mind, ou can always lick it off.) This strange fact is due either o colour-blindness on the part of the treacle makers, or lse the treacle changes colour when it's in the tin, which eems most unlikely.

Why not discuss this absurd situation with your parents nd relations, telling them that it's part of a scientific xperiment. Have them test the treacle like you did. Then *hey'll* get all covered with sticky treacle as well. (That will revent your being told off for getting in such a mess.)

The reason for doing all these daft things is to prove to yourself how useful this book can be – for broadening the mind, adding to your intelligence and awakening your brain – if you read it carefully. And, what's more important, it'll help you to find ways to eat lots of nice sticky sweet things.

Now for the next exercise. Look closely at the Red Sea. (Or a colour photograph of it.) Just what do you see when you see this sea . . . ?

The Red Sea isn't red – it's blue.

Peers of the Realm can't be arrested for civil offences, but they can be for treason or felony.

In China, a man can divorce his wife for being a chatterbox.

The capacity of the human stomach is about five pints.

There is no such thing as a living sardine. The true sardine is a fish which has been cured and preserved.

It's impossible to fold a piece of paper – no matter how big it is – more than seven times.

Gorillas can't swim.

If a thoughtless neighbour has his radio turned up too loud, you can easily get your own back. Find the frequency of the AM station he is listening to, subtract 460, and dial your own radio to this new number. Yours doesn't even have to be turned up; his radio will start to squeal intolerably and he'll most likely turn it off.

On the 24th August, 1918, in Hendon, near Sunderland, it rained eels for ten minutes. The fish covered about half an acre.

Boxer Rocky Marciano has the same birthday as the late heavyweight champion James J. Corbett – 1st September.

Most Eskimos use refrigerators – to keep their food from freezing.

There are 509 different species of water-bug in England.

Camels do not carry water or food stored in their humps. All the hump contains is fat.

The surname 'Fortnum' means 'A strong, young, tail-less donkey'.

Although the death penalty for murder no longer exists in England, there are still three crimes for which hanging is the penalty. They are Treason; Arson in a naval dockyard; and Piracy with violence.

Rice paper isn't made from rice, but from a small tree of the ivy family grown in Formosa.

The first organised 'strike' of workers dates back to 309 B.C. Then Aristos, a Greek musician, called out his orchestra because they weren't allowed to have their meals in the temple.

Westminster Abbey isn't an Abbey at all. It is the Collegiate Church of St Peter in the county of Middlesex.

Dick Turpin, the famous highwayman, never rode from London to York in a day, despite the legend. The distance of 200 miles would have taken him at least five days to accomplish.

The spider isn't an insect. It belongs to the arachnid family.

In 1851, a Scottish Archer in South Uist, Robert Kilpatrick, shot an egg from his son's head at 100 yards. He also had a second arrow in his belt ready for his Chief, William MacDonald, who had ordered him to attempt the shot.

The word 'school' comes from the Greek word 'Schole' – which, literally translated, means 'Leisure'.

The average person changes position anywhere from between 20 to 65 times in the course of a night's sleep.

Edgar Allan Poe, the master horror writer, wrote all his stories with his black cat 'Magic' sitting on his shoulder.

Fear of quicksand is unfounded. If you can swim in water, you can swim in quicksand, and even if you can't, there's still no worry. Quicksand is just sand and water, and its specific gravity is so high that at least a quarter of you will remain above the surface.

Feeling a temptation to neglect his scholarly duties, the Greek philosopher Demosthenes shaved one side of his head, so he'd feel too humiliated to be seen in public.

The ancient Egyptians invented the basis of modern shorthand more than 1,700 years ago.

The longest-named railway station in the world is in North Wales. It is:

LLANFAIRPWLLGWYNGYLLGOGORYCHWYRNDROBWLLLLAN-TYSILIOGOGOCH.

(The station's nameplate, by the way, is 26 yards long.)

The most efficient form of light production known to man is attributed to the glow-worm.

During the 1968 mayoral election in Picoaza, Equador, a foot powder known as 'Pulverpise' ran an advertising campaign with the slogan: 'Vote for any candidate, but if you want well-being and hygiene, vote for "Pulverpise"!' When the votes were all in and had been counted, 'Pulverpise' had been elected Mayor of Picoaza.

Although it's popularly thought to be, the leek isn't the official national emblem of Wales. It's a daffodil.

Postal deliveries in La Florida, Venezuela, came to a halt in 1972 when the postman's horse died. Officials went on record as saying that they had no plans to buy another horse.

Spanish scientists are boosting milk production for dairy farmers by fitting stainless steel dentures to cows. With a set of false teeth, chewing the cud becomes more of a pleasure for cattle whose own teeth are in poor condition. The cows' milk yield has soared by up to 70 per cent.

Turkish baths aren't Turkish – and they aren't baths, either. They are simply rooms filled with hot air and were invented by the early Romans.

The human race, according to scientists at the University of California, is now one thousand million years old. Happy birthday.

The name of King Ethelred the Unready doesn't mean that he was never ready. On the contrary. The word in Old English was 'Unrede' from 'Redeless' and meant 'Always waiting in Counsel'.

Wallpaper was first used as a decoration for Chinese tombs.

Black treacle – which is called green treacle on the tin it is sold in – is neither of the colours, but is actually brown.

The first hand-grenade containing gun powder was invented by the Mongol leader, Khubla Khan, in 1230.

How to be Top
of the Class

If you're something of a dunce at lessons, don't sulk or go around hiding people's shoelaces for revenge. There's hope for you yet. You can be top of the class if you learn enough curious information from these pages and use it properly. What you must learn to do is play the game called 'Confuse The Teacher'.

Here's how to play the game. When your teacher asks you a very difficult question, such as 'What are fifteen times seventy-eight?', don't start working it out in your head, panic, give up, then remain silent. The teacher will think you're stupid. Instead, say something like: 'Before I answer that, sir, can you tell me if it's true that the haggis was invented by the Ancient Greeks?' There's a good chance that the teacher will be so astonished and confused

39

that he'll mark your answer correct, then pass on to an easier victim to torture with his horrible sums.

Other ways of announcing startling facts to teachers include:

'As you are an expert on science, sir, perhaps you can confirm the fact that . . .'

'Sir, did you know that . . .'

'Look, sir! On the ceiling! A ladybird – which, you may be interested to know . . .'

'That's a difficult sentence to write, sir. Which reminds me of the longest sentence ever written. Do you know it, sir . . . ?'

Here in this chapter you'll find a pirate's horde of suitable curious facts to confuse teachers with, and to raise you from dunce-status.

The word 'News', when associated with newspapers, or news in general, is derived from the four points of the compass: i.e. N—E—W—S.

Stilton cheese isn't made in Stilton, but in the vale of Belvoir, Leicestershire.

When the Russian writer Tolstoy (author of *War and Peace*) was a boy, he formed an exclusive club with his brother. To be initiated, a member had to stand in a corner of the room for an hour and not think of a white bear.

The renowned 'New Bridge' (*Pont Neuf*) in Paris is in fact the oldest bridge in the city.

By choosing the correct starting point, it is possible to go due south from Arkansas, U.S.A., into each of the adjoining six states.

The expression 'Blind as a bat' is sheer nonsense. Bats aren't blind at all. Neither are moles.

The word 'cleave' has two definitions – 'to split or cut apart' and 'to cling or hold together'.

Holidaymakers by the sea often praise the healthy ozone in the air. They're mistaken – what they can smell is just decaying seaweed. Ozone isn't present below an altitude of seven thousand feet.

Haggis is not of Scottish origin. It was invented by the Ancient Greeks, who called it *Koila Prodateia*.

Most people think the heart is on the left side of the body. It isn't. Nine-tenths of it is on the right side.

Earwigs never creep into peoples ears. The name dates from Anglo-Saxon times, when 'ear' meant an 'undeveloped flower bud', where the insect liked to hide.

Acute nasopharyngitis

If your doctor tells you you're suffering from acute nasopharyngitis, don't worry. That's the scientific name for the common cold.

Magnesium gains weight in the process of burning; it's ashes weigh more than the metal itself.

Henry VIII's second wife, Anne Boleyn, always wore gloves to hide an odd physical deformity. She had six fingers on her left hand.

The poodle doesn't moult.

Lions used to be kept (as ferocious guard-dogs) in the Tower of London up till 1781.

The very first lightning conductor was put up by Prohop Dilwish in Morovia in 1754.

The largest hamburger ever cooked was 14 feet in circumference, and it contained 173 lb of beef. It was made i Yagona, Australia, in 1972.

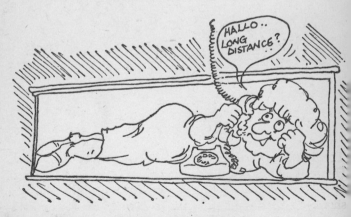

The famous spiritualist Amy Semple MacPherson was buried with a live telephone in her coffin.

The elephant is the only animal that cannot jump. On the other hand, it is the only animal that can be taught to stand on its head.

The longest sentence ever published appears in Victor Hugo's *Les Misérables*. It is 823 words long and takes up over three pages. Hugo, among others, also wrote the shortest letter on record. While on holiday, he was anxious to find out how *Les Misérables* was selling. To his Paris publishers he wrote: '?' The reply was '!'.

The only hotel in the world with a solid gold bath is Funabara on the Isu peninsula, Japan. It costs one pound to have a two minute soak in this bath, which is worth £150,000.

The highest waterfall in the world is not the Niagara Falls, but the Kaietur Falls in British Guiana. They are 741 feet high; nearly five times the height of Niagara.

The word 'Unquestionably' contains all the five vowels.

The English classical composer Vaughan Williams wrote a concerto for the mouth-organ.

Mice can actually sing. Their songs, when magnified, resemble the twitterings of a canary, and are very musical.

In Arabia, ants are kept as pets, mainly to get rid of the termites and other wood-eating bugs in the houses.

Teddy bears were named in honour of the American president Theodore Roosevelt.

Cleopatra's Needle, on the Victoria Embankment in London, has nothing whatsoever to do with Cleopatra. Hieroglyphics, carved on the obelisk, tell that it was first erected in Egypt in 1475 B.C. – over 14 centuries before Cleopatra was born.

Cows have five stomachs.

St Andrew, Scotland's patron saint, wasn't a Scot at all. He was a Pict, a race that was regarded as Scotland's greatest enemy.

A war fought between England and Zanzibar, which begun on the 27th August 1896, lasted just 38 minutes.

Sultan Selim III of Turkey fired an arrow 972 yards in 1798.

A person breathes, on average, approximately 17 times a minute.

German silver contains no silver at all. It is an alloy of copper, zinc and nickel.

A Spanish explorer lost in the jungles of South America in 1821 decided, rather than starve to death, to end it all by eating the root of the bitter and poisonous Casaver plant. He boiled the roots in water and drank the concoction. Nothing happened. He'd accidentally discovered a new food, and it was given a South American Indian name: Tapioca.

Don't Look Now, but it's Fried Grasshoppers for Lunch

This chapter is mainly concerned with the fads and fashions of the day. For, example, it used to be a fashion to hang pudding basins on the very tops of church spires. But that's out of date now. Today, to show your daring and quick wit, you'll have to scale a spire in a raging blizzard, and hang up a flag with an amazing piece of curious information embroidered on it, such as: 'It is against the law to eat snakes on Sunday in Iraq!' Other suitably sensational facts can be found in the following pages.

Also to be found here is valuable advice that will help your mother, or sister, or girlfriend, or boyfriend, if they're on a slimming diet. When they sit down to eat, inform them: 'Do you realise that a serving of fish and fried grasshoppers contains only 235 calories!' This will most certainly make them feel very sick, and they won't feel like eating *anything*. So they'll lose even more weight, and be so pleased that they might well reward you for your help. (Don't play this trick too often, though, or they'll grow smaller and smaller – and eventually disappear altogether!)

Now set to and study the facts, and before long you'll be regarded as an expert on fads and fashions. Or at least you'll end up with an extra dinner or two.

Belgian scientists have invented an awesome digestion machine which turns the cellulose in scrap paper and cardboard into sugar and imitation maple-syrup.

There *was* such a person as John O'Groats. He was a farmer who lived on Ducansby Head, the northernmost part of Scotland, in the 16th century.

Alaska was once sold to America by Russia in 1867 for the sum of £4 million. (Worth about £35 million today.)

The first recorded appearance of a slot-machine was in the ancient temples of Alexandria. There were machines there from which a supply of Holy Water could be obtained when a coin was inserted in them – this was back in 641 BC.

A person suffering from oikophobia is somebody who has a morbid dread of being at home.

In the very first story about Cinderella (published in France in 1844), her glass slipper was not made of glass – but of fur. And Cinderella's real name was 'Ash Mail'.

Woodpecker scalps were highly prized by North American Indian tribes – one was enough to buy a wife with.

A travel book presented to Queen Victoria was two and a half feet thick, four feet tall and weighed 88 lb.

Asbestos and asphalt might be thought to be modern inventions, but they aren't. Both were discovered and used by the Sumerians in Mesopotamia as long ago as 3500 B.C.

The great fire of London in 1666 was started in a baker's shop in Pudding Lane, by a careless boy who threw a match into a box of straw.

The word 'tip' derives from the initial letters of the words 'To Insure Promptness', which were often printed above a box set in a convenient place in 17th century inns.

George the First, King of England from 1714 to 1727, was German and couldn't speak a word of English.

'Aesop's Fables' weren't written by Aesop. Aesop was a deformed Phrygian slave of the 6th century B.C. Many of the fables attributed to him have been discovered on Egyptian papyre of 1,000 years earlier.

Modern whalers use the mammal's liver as a bag to carry their golf clubs in.

The funny bone isn't a bone. It is a nerve, which, rather appropriately, is located near the humerus bone in the arm.

Although it's accepted that Eve tempted Adam with an apple in the Garden of Eden, it's not mentioned in the Bible story. All it says is that it was 'the fruit of a forbidden tree'. And according to ancient Mohammedan tradition, the 'forbidden tree' was a fig tree.

The Kirghiz tribe in Asia forbids a woman to utter her husband's name. The penalty for doing so is instant divorce.

There is such a thing as a 'Ha-ha'! It is an ancient boundary ditch.

The common 52-card pack, developed by a Frenchman in 1392, symbolises the calendar:

52 cards – number of weeks in a year.
4 suits – the four seasons.
13 cards in a suit – number of weeks in a season.
Red and Black – day and night.

(Playing cards, incidentally, were invented in Hindustan in the early 7th century.)

One serving of fish and two fried grasshoppers contains a total of 235 calories.

The leaning tower of Pisa is supposed to be unique, but the temple Church at Bristol leans just as much (7 feet out of the perpendicular).

It is forbidden to send red envelopes through the post. The only exception is when the letter is addressed to the renter of a private box for night use and is marked 'Private Box – Night Delivery'.

The smallest prison in the British Isles is on the Isle of Sark. It can hold only two prisoners at a time.

The Chinese language contains no 'R' sounds; so the Chinese substitute the 'L' sound for English words. On the other hand, the Japanese language has no 'L' sound; they substitute an 'R' sound. Thus in Chinese, 'Fry' is pronounced 'Fly' – and in Japanese, the word 'Fly' is pronounced 'Fry'.

It is against the law to eat snakes on Sunday in Iraq.

Forgers of banknotes use up to a dozen eggs per note to give the dud money the authentic texture and colour.

The famous model T Ford cars (nicknamed 'The Tin Lizzie') which were first produced in 1908, cost £59 to buy new.

Brigham Young, American Mormon leader, once married four women in one day.

A racehorse can be a 'one-year-old' just a few minutes after its birth. This is because it becomes one year old on January 1st following its birth – so if it's born just before midnight on December the 31st, it gains a whole year.

The giraffe has the same number of bones in its neck as a human being.

The average range of the human voice under normal conditions is approximately 150 yards. But at night, across an expanse of still water, it can reach to 300 yards.

Thomas Young, the 18th century physician, mathematician and scientist, could speak twelve languages fluently at the age of eight.

The exact centre of England is Meridan Cross, Warwickshire.

More than 200 members of the audience in Australia's new £50 million Sydney opera house have no view of the stage.

The 'Black Maria' police van, used for taking prisoners from the Courts to prison, is named after Mrs Maria Manning. With the help of her husband she murdered their lodger, and was executed at Horsemonger Lane jail at Southwark in 1849 – wearing heavy black clothing for the occasion.

Julius Caesar wasn't a Roman Emperor – in fact there was no Roman Empire till a long time after his death. He was Consul five times, and was made a Dictator.

Where and When to Use Fantastic and Curious Facts

Don't let the amazing bits of information you've learned from this book stay locked in your head all the time. Let them out for some fresh air! Try not to think of them as mere scraps of curious knowledge, but rather as friends who can come to your aid in moments of danger of embarrassment. Think of them as tools, with which you can make moments of wonder and beauty out of nothing. Think of them as brightly gleaming weapons, that can be flashed through the air to demolish evil foes, slay fire-breathing dragons, and rescue beautiful damsels in distress . . .

Well, perhaps that is going a bit *too* far. But do remember that the facts are capable of great things. And there's a time and a place to use them to their best effect – and to their worst effect. (Both the same thing, really.)

On the following pages are listed several of the many moments and situations when the fantastic facts could come to your help, save the day, while away idle moments, or even make you a hero of the day.

Use Fantastic Information . . .

. . .During a boring tour of St Paul's Cathedral or Westminster Abbey.

. . . While listening to static or interference on the radio.

. . . When you're waiting for an interview with an angry headmaster.

. . . While watching a Russian film with Polish sub-titles.

. . . When your bicycle chain falls off and you can't find the missing link.

. . . As space-fillers in the blanks on your History Exam papers.

. . . While swimming the English Channel.

. . . During the school production of *As You Like It*.

. . . Between the grooves of a warped record.

. . . When Chelsea are losing 5–0 at half time, and you've lost your programme.

Use Fantastic Information . . .

. . . To help pass away the time *between* the commercials on television.

. . . On Census forms when nobody is looking.

. . . To stop yourself thinking about being sea-sick.

. . . To confuse 'Information' Desk Clerks at railway stations.

. . . When watching that annoying test-card on television.

. . . In place of eating liquorice allsorts when you've no money.

. . . If a stranger asks you the way.

. . . While listening to any operatic singer.

. . . To wake up a dying conversation. (Or else to kill it once and for all.)

. . . For your 'most-worthless-child-in-the-class' prize speech, if you're asked.

Use Fantastic Information . . .

. . . When you find a horse in the horse-radish sauce.

. . . In the competition entry forms on the back of cereal boxes and in the newspapers.

. . . To impress your pet dog (or pet giraffe).

. . . When you want to annoy your teacher and get sent out of the classroom.

... To revive unconscious pot-plants.

... As unusual Christmas presents for your parents.

... If you're discovered up a tree scrumping apples.

... If you forget the words when reciting Kipling's poem *If*.

... To enliven your composition on 'What You Did In The Holidays'.

... If you're captured and held prisoner by a gang of ruthless Russian secret agents.

Use Fantastic Information . . .

. . . When your trousers fall down.

. . . As blackmail to get more pocket-money when your father's just about to watch his favourite television programme.

. . . To wash your neck with.

. . . When your girl-friend (or boy-friend) tells you she (or he) has counted the spots on your face and the total is a hundred and four.

... If you meet a man from Mars.

...And most important:
USE FANTASTIC INFORMATION ...
... To change the subject!

(Come to think of it, that's not such a bad idea. Let's change the chapter!)

The Amazing Perpetual
Calendar and Other Games

Wouldn't it be jolly to find out exactly which day of the week you were born on? Well, perhaps it wouldn't. But you must admit that this kind of curious knowledge is appealing, and unique. So featuring in this jolly chapter is an elaborate chart, called 'The Perpetual Calendar'. Careful study of this chart will enable you to find out the weekday of any day since the year dot. Just as long as you know the date – whether it's that of Julius Caesar's birthday, when the Great Fire of London started, or your birthday or your friends' – you'll be able to find out on which day of the week it occurred.

Attached to this chart is the old nursery rhyme that begins: 'Monday's child is full of . . .' etc., so you can discover what sort of person you are. Also in this chapter you'll meet the breathtaking 'Magic Age' table. This cunning device will mystify your friends, make your enemies disappear with envy, and cause many adults to look upon you as a child-genius (which of course you are – otherwise you wouldn't be reading this book!)

So relax and enjoy this chapter while you may. For the chapter after it is a real death-defying quiz, the like of which has never been seen on this planet before, dead or alive.

The Amazing Perpetual Calendar

(*To Find the Weekday of any Date in the Christian Era*)

Add together the following numbers:

(1) The number of the year.

(2) The result (omitting fractions) of dividing the number of the year by 4.

(3) Six times the number of completed centuries.

(4) The result (omitting fractions) of dividing the number of completed centuries by 4.

(5) The Index Number of the month from Table ONE

(6) The number of the day of the month.

Then divide the total by 7. The Remainder will give you the day of the week according to Table TWO.

(An example of how all this is done is given after the two tables.)

Table 1

MONTH	INDEX NUMBER
January	0
January (In Leap Year)	6
February	3
February (In Leap Year)	2
March	3
April	6
May	1
June	4
July	6
August	2
September	5
October	0
November	3
December	5

(Note: A year is a leap year if its number is exactly divisible by 4, unless its number ends in 00. In this case it is only a leap year if the preceding figures form a number divisible by 4. Thus 1600 and 2000 are leap years; 1800 and 1900 are not.)

Table 2

Remainder	Day of Week
1	Sunday
2	Monday
3	Tuesday
4	Wednesday
5	Thursday
6	Friday
7	Saturday.

EXAMPLE:

What was the day of the week on the 9th of July, 1930?

1.	Number of the year	1930
2.	Number after division by 4	482
3.	Number of completed centuries is 19. 6 × 19	114
4.	Number after dividing 19 by 4	4
5.	Index Number from Table ONE for July	6
6.	Day of the month	9

Total	2545
Divide by 7	363
Remainder	4

From Table TWO, the day of the week is Wednesday.

What Kind of Person Are You?

From using this Perpetual Calendar, you can find out on what day of the week you were born. There's an old nursery rhyme, invented by an unknown poet hundreds of years ago, that is supposed to tell you what your character is from the day of the week on which you were born. Here's how it goes:

MONDAY's child is fair of face;

TUESDAY's child is full of grace;

WEDNESDAY's child is full of woe;

THURSDAY's child has far to go;

FRIDAY's child is loving and giving;

SATURDAY's child works hard for a living;

But the child who's born on the Sabbath day (SUNDAY),
Is bonny and blythe and good and gay.

(Let's hope you weren't born on a Wednesday. If you
were, cast aside your woes, leap upon your toes, beam a
bright smile and astound all in sight with the astonish-
ing . . .

THE AMAZING MAGIC AGE TABLE

Here's a mysterious and magic age table that will mystify everybody you meet when you show it to them. Ask them to look at it carefully, and tell you in which columns their ages appear. Within seconds you'll be able to tell them exactly how old they are.

How do you do it? Simple as eating a doughnut. Just add together the numbers at the beginning of the columns in which their ages are shown. And that's it.

Here's an example: If someone is 17, the number 17 appears in the first and the fifth column. The first numbers in these columns are 1 and 16. Add them together and you get the correct age – 17. Now copy the Magic Age Table on to a separate sheet of paper and set forth to mystify and astound the world. (But don't go too far and get lost – you have that devil of a Quiz to do in the next chapter yet!)

Magic Age Tables

1	2	4	8	16	32
3	3	5	9	17	33
5	6	6	10	18	34
7	7	7	11	19	35
9	10	12	12	20	36
11	11	13	13	21	37
13	14	14	14	22	38
15	15	15	15	23	39
17	18	20	24	24	40
19	19	21	25	25	41
21	22	22	26	26	42
23	23	23	27	27	43
25	26	28	28	28	44
27	27	29	29	29	45
29	30	30	30	30	46
31	31	31	31	31	47
33	34	36	40	48	48
35	35	37	41	49	49
37	38	38	42	50	50
39	39	39	43	51	51
41	42	44	44	52	52
43	43	45	45	53	53
45	46	46	46	54	54
47	47	47	47	55	55
49	50	52	56	56	56
51	51	53	57	57	57
53	54	54	58	58	58
55	55	55	59	59	59
57	58	60	60	60	60
59	59	61	61	61	61
61	62	62	62	62	62
63	63	63	63	63	63

84

Know Your C.I.Q.

(Curiosity Intelligence Quotient)

Those smart guys and girls are always bragging about how high their I.Q. is. Well, let them. With this unique book as your guide, you can brag about how high your C.I.Q. is. (*Curiosity* Intelligence Quotient.) That'll make the teacher's pets whine with jealousy.

But before you go around bragging, first you'd better check to see that you have learned a lot of curious and amazing information from these peculiar pages. That's why the following quiz is here, ready and waiting for your pencil.

The quiz comes in two parts. In the first, you choose and answer from the given selection. In the second part you have to answer true or false to the statements given.

The correct answers are to be found at the back of the book. (If they're not there, then they've got lost. If this is the case you can mark all your answers correct and feel on top of the world for days.)

But the answers will probably be there, along with a scoring chart that tells you how well or woefully you did. Now go ahead, and good luck. Mind you don't cheat, or a magic genie might pop out of the book and eat you.

Part One

The Choice Is Yours

1. Who invented the Nobel Peace prize?
   (a) Junius Caterpillar Inkpen
   (b) Adolf Hitler
   (c) Atilla the Hun
   (d) Alfred B. Nobel

2. 'Ju Jitsu', literally translated, means:
   (a) 'Get off my head!'
   (b) 'The gentle art'
   (c) 'There are eleven kippers in my wardrobe'
   (d) 'My grandfather is in the wardrobe'

3. How old was Mozart when he composed 'Twinkle Twinkle Little Star'?

(a) Two months and a day

(b) Five years

(c) Ninety-two years

(d) Fifty years

4. What have jumping beans got inside them?

(a) Bloater paste sandwiches

(b) Smaller jumping beans

(c) Live fleas

(d) Goblins

5. Where is it illegal to eat snakes on Sunday?

(a) Battersea Dogs Home

(b) Iraq

(c) Tahiti

(d) On top of Big Ben

6. What is acute Nasopharyngitis?

(a) A very pretty summer dress

(b) Roller-skates with built in stereo

(c) The common cold

(d) A ladder without any rungs

7. Who invented the haggis?

(a) The ancient Greeks

(b) Celtic football club

(c) Alfred Haggis

(d) Alexander the Great

8. What physical deformity did Anne Boleyn have?

(a) She had a long green beard

(b) She had no toes

(c) She had eleven ears

(d) She had six fingers on her left hand

9. Where is London's Petticoat Lane market held?

(a) High Street, Calcutta

(b) Middlesex Street

(c) Epping Forest

(d) The River Thames

10. What animals were used as guard dogs in the Tower of London?

(a) Otters

(b) Kangaroos

(c) Piglets

(d) Lions

Part Two

True – or False?

(Just mark 'T' or 'F' against each statement)

1. Amy Semple McPherson was buried with a live rhinocerous in her coffin.

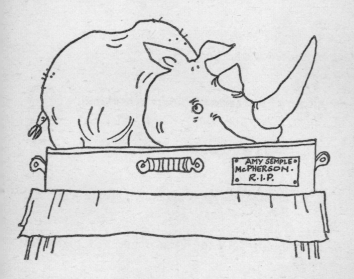

2. Mice can sing melodies.

3. Teddy bears were named in honour of Teddy boys.

4. Elephants can jump over ten feet high.

5. St Andrew wasn't Scottish.

6. An ostrich egg takes five hours to hard-boil.

7. Bulls cannot tell one colour from another.

8. A person breathes approximately 17 times a minute.

9. King Louis XIV of France invented high-heeled shoes.

10. A fly's wings vibrate 340 times a second.

11. Deers have two gall bladders.

12. Stilton cheese is made in Japan.

13. There is no lead in a lead pencil.

14. The heart is on the left side of the body.

15. People in Turkey wear violet-coloured clothes to mourn the dead.

16. The motto of the Salvation Army is: 'Let's Play Football!'

17. Cows have two stomachs.

18. Bats can see in the dark.

19. Snakes hear through their jaws.

20. The human voice can be heard from 300 yards away.

Answers

Part One

1. *d;* 2. *b;* 3. *b;* 4. *c;* 5. *b;* 6. *c;* 7. *a;* 8. *d;* 9. *b;* 10. *d.*

Part Two

1. False; 2. True; 3. False; 4. False; 5. True; 6. False;
7. True; 8. True; 9. True; 10. True; 11. False; 12. False;
13. True; 14. False; 15. True; 16. False; 17. False; 18.
True; 19. False; 20. True.

Scoring Chart

None correct:
Are you quite sure you *did* the quiz? Perhaps you're suffering from loss of memory. You're obviously suffering from *something*. It might be a good idea if you had a quiet lie down in a dark room for a few years.

1–5 correct:
Not a bad little effort. Next time, however, try taking the cap of your pen off before starting the quiz.

6–10 correct:
Reasonable. The trouble is you're too well informed on ordinary, practical subjects. Try again.

11–20 *correct:*
A very good result, indicating that you have strong powers of memory and a weak sense of judgement.

21–28 *correct:*
You cheated. Here comes that hungry genie now . . .

30 *correct:*
The winner! You can take pride in the fact that you're stuffed full of Curious Information. Your high C.I.Q. will take you far . . . Whether or not it will bring you back alive is another question. A question that can only be answered by further study of this book, which will lead you into complete chaos, which will bring you back to the first chapter of the book again.